The METHOD A
Best kept hidden secret revealed

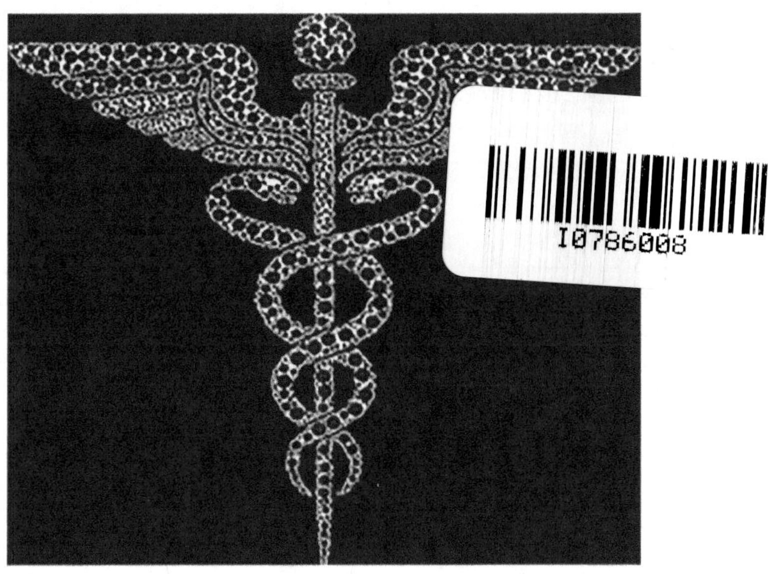

Unique, Innovative and New

Not found anywhere

Boost recovery results by 50%

Easy fast steps to do NOW

Hamish N Ramdharry

Disclaimer:

No part of this eBook or book may be reproduced or transmitted in any form or by any means, electronic or mechanical, including photocopying, recording or by any information storage and retrieval system, without written permission from the author.

The information provided within this Book is for general informational purposes only. The methods described within this Book are the author's personal thoughts shaped by industry experts.
They are not intended to be a definitive set of instructions for this project.
You may discover there are other methods and materials to accomplish the same result.

While we try to keep the information up-to-date and correct, there are no representations or warranties, express or implied, about the completeness, accuracy, reliability, suitability or availability with respect to the information, products, services, or related graphics contained in this Book for any purpose. Any use of this information is at your own risk.

This book is not intended to be a substitute for the medical advice of a licensed physician. The reader should consult with their doctor in any matters relating to his/her health.

Parts of the book has been reproduced with permission from the authors.
Cover picture by pixabay.com (Free vector graphic)

I would like to extend special thanks to Sobhunand Seeparsad and Eshan Auchoybur. Your help and assistance is greatly appreciated in putting this book together.

Published and authored by Hamish Ramdharry 2018

For any queries please contact me on Instagram: hamishramdharry

Mind Exercises To Help Overcome Depression, Anxiety and Fear

INTRODUCTION

Have you bought and read books, followed any therapy, or taken pills and still made zero progress?

Do you feel resigned and forced to live like this out of powerlessness?

Are you wondering how this manual differs from everything else?

Does the sound of a never seen before unpublished technique that bring results interest you?

Well, I think you have come to the right place. This book, or call it friendly advisory techniques, will deliver a potential solution to assist you to overcome anxiety, depression and fear.

First, I must confess that the traditional treatments and self-help literature did not help me. Through extensive research and a combination of scientific disciplines, I believe that I have finally found an easy and lasting method to take control of my condition. I find my method second to none as I have not crossed anything like it in the anxiety and depression literature available.

This unique approach will help you boost your chances of recovery, reveal fiercely guarded secrets in the psychological fields, and transform your relationship with anxiety, depression and fear.

The research is not revelatory, as the areas that I cover are widely known, and yet, I am surprised that till now, no specialists in the discipline have these techniques published into one easy to use manual.

The Method I propose could be the game changer that will change your life. By applying these easy to follow steps you can increase your recovery chances by at least 50%

I must confess that I do have moments of anxiety and depression, but I know when I feel this way and by applying The METHOD A I know exactly what to do to push it into the background.

The METHOD A has restored my sanity and my life has changed for the better. It will do the same for you.

Table of contents:

1

Do you own a mobile smartphone? If yes, then this will make sense to you.

Anxiety and depression is not an illness. I repeat, there is nothing wrong with you. You are biologically perfect, and you are growing every day just like everyone else.
Yet deep down, lurking in the shadows there is something holding you back leaving an overwhelming sense of fear.

You try to mentally isolate the concern to find a solution, but instead you are mercilessly bombarded by negative thoughts and unnecessary chatter leaving you frustrated, powerless, and emotionally exhausted.

In some severe cases, your frustration turns to anger which eventually leads to fear and as a result, your self-worth, self-confidence, and self-esteem begins to erode.

This is where things get muddy. There is a tipping point, where the erosion becomes so acute, that you unknowingly reformat your mental state to operate on a basis of fear. It is at this junction where anxiety and depression sets in.

Your mind will now look for problems in everyday life, and when you are left to your thoughts, all you can think about are problems that happened in your past, problems that may occur in the present, and run probable scenarios of problems in the future.

If all you think about are problems, and how to problem solve, then you are not focusing on how to plan ahead to achieve the things that you want and to live on your terms.

For example, you are using a mobile application to check the weather app to see which would be the hottest day to go to the beach.

A healthy mind will think about the beautiful ocean, the brightness of the clear blue sky, the warmth of the sun on their skin, the gentle lapping of the waves, the sense of peace while lying on the beach. The phone is a tool to gather the information to meet a goal.

A person with anxiety and depression will think about the following. What if my phone doesn't work, what if the app crashes, what if the weather turns out to be rainy, and what if there are no modes of transport, what if I get sunburnt, and so on.
The phone itself becomes a problem, and then the mind begins to troubleshoot every possible detail of the trip.

The mind is programmed to find problems with the goal of going to the beach. Once at the beach, surely the mind will look out for more problems rather than enjoy the moment.

Both have similar goals, both have a mobile phone, however the difference is in the mind.
One is full of hope and see's the goal. The image in their mind is vivid and they begin to look forward.

The other is riddled with worry seeing only the problems losing sight of the goal. The image in their mind is not vivid and a sense of fear creeps in.

Imagine a mobile smart phone loaded with wonderful applications. How many times have you been asked to carry out updates on the application?

     Do you own a mobile smartphone? If yes, then this will make sense to you.

The phone remains the same, the application is only ever downloaded once, and yet there are regular updates to ensure that the application runs optimally.

These new updates come from the developers who use client feedback to improve the application.

We must view our minds in a similar fashion. The phone is our mind, the application is the way we formulate our thoughts which is now on a fear based setting, and we now require regular updates to ensure that our thoughts run optimally and deliberately.

If this is the case, then surely a step towards overcoming anxiety and depression would be to install a non-fear, anxious, and depressed mental framework as the application and make regular updates to our mental software.

Our approach to life is based on experiences and lessons learned. It guides the way we conduct ourselves in the future and how we interpret the external environment as we grow. To an extent some of the experience will be helpful as we can draw upon past examples to decipher the present situation.

However, we cannot simply apply the established rules because the circumstances and environment have changed. The rules may no longer be applicable.

For example, the rules in a teenage relationship do not equally apply to a marriage, the way we lived in a rented accommodation would not be the same when owning a house, saving for a holiday would not be the same when you have a family holiday.

As life unfolds, we are exposed to increasing levels of life complexities, and to overcome challenges we apply personally established and developed rules and principles. We are convinced that what we have learned in the past will be sufficient and adequate to tackle future problems.

Instead of trying to learn new lessons and mentally update past experiences, people with anxiety and depression continually and stubbornly apply their outdated thinking to a new and completely different environment.
If at first, we don't succeed, then we try harder! No matter how many times we fail, we still keep at it until we become mentally drained and frustrated.

The established rules are not applicable and when results do not manifest, the person loses more self-confidence, self-worth and self-esteem and anxiety and depression takes root.

These established rules formed during our teenage years, have allowed our teenage belief system to dictate our behaviour and thinking in an adult belief system.
The biggest difference between the two is that in an adult system, the adult mind is one that does not react immediately to external events, and secondly, builds upon past experience.

2

Which one best describes your choice of thinking so far?

Those with an adult mind-set have a set of clearly defined personal goals and ambitions in life.

They have a mental framework for their vision and know how to achieve this vision.

The adult mind applies its goal-setting and problem-solving abilities to an external event and then responds in a manner that serves the realisation of their grand vision.

Those with anxiety and depression have weaker goal-setting and problem-solving traits.

Rather than assessing external events based on whether it serves their grand vision, they instead react out of fear by displaying any of the following traits: fight, flight, freeze or fix.

When a person instinctively operates from a place of fear they only see conflict as they have no clear goals to aspire to. Therefore, they instead engage in defending their self-worth, self-confidence and self-esteem by any means necessary based on the 4Fs. It is the protection of self, rather than a positive engagement to the situation. These four responses lack maturity of thought and will not lead to adult solutions.

They feel that they are at the mercy of situations and must constantly fight or defend themselves rather than accept the situation as it is.

They will either seek or avoid conflict, remain neutral or try to fix the conflict to protect their own vulnerabilities and insecurities regardless of the consequences.

Mentally armed with their four approaches to situations, they shoot first and ask questions later, and to stop the constant battle from life they seek to control the situation in the hope to bear some influence on the outcome.

Anxious people worry that life exposes their vulnerabilities and as their self-esteem, self-confidence and self-worth are low they will lack the confidence in their ability to deal with new situations.
Because they believe that they lack the ability, they then look for another way to neutralise perceived threats.
This sense of powerlessness then forces the person to try and control the environments they find themselves in.
As you can imagine, there is no way that you can control life and once again they find themselves back to square one.

As soon as a threat (imagined or real) is identified, it is swiftly dealt by one of the four approaches and the mental search for another perceived threat begins.

The mind has now been trained to look out for negatives to protect ones' core values, i.e. self-esteem, self-worth and self-confidence.

3

Do you believe in happily ever after? I did and regretted it immediately.

Anxious people hold a belief that there exists an ever-lasting solution to be free from hurt and fear.

E.g. If I had money all my problems will go away, or if only if I had this then I could do that and then I will be worry free, and even, if only I had the same advantages of rich and connected people then I would not have a care in the world.

They will relentlessly seek a 'one solution fits all' to their perceived or real worries, and will not stop until they find it. They either blame themselves or others for their shortcomings, and apply the 4Fs in the hope of preserving any self-worth, confidence and esteem until they find that elusive solution.

Meanwhile a non-anxious person is not mentally driven by the urge to protect their core values, but instead their aim is to boost their core values. Rather than protect what they have, these people build upon what they have. This is personal growth.

They will identify and assess the situation, take stock of any potential opportunities, and then act in a way that serves their values and interests. The mature mind seeks to identify opportunities that meets their life goals and vision as this will give them the healthy confidence and self-esteem levels required to live without anxiety and depression.

They also identify threats, but they only spend sufficient resources to neutralise them, and the majority of resources is invested into their vision.

In contrast, anxious people spend little time on constructive thoughts to move forward towards their goals and ambitions, they instead spend too much mental effort on the negatives and hardly any quality time on the opportunities that leads to their specific goals. They seek a solution that makes our world threat free.

The opposite of anxiety and depression is high self-confidence, self-worth and self-esteem.
The higher the anxiety and depression, the lower the self-confidence, self-worth and self-esteem.
So, it would make sense to therefore boost self-confidence, self-worth and self-esteem in order break the grip of anxiety and depression.

Let me tell you know, there is no happily after!

Nothing stays perfect and things will always go wrong or requires tweaking. Life is dynamic and every new situation, moment and second requires a different response.
This can be very frustrating let us be honest. It is no surprise that we are riddled with worry and anxiety, as there can be no over-riding formula for a trouble, threat free life.

Until they do find that elusive solution, an anxious person will manage their fears by attempting to seize control of a situation to influence the outcome.
Physiologist Walter Bradford Cannon coined the term fight or flight response. He explained that it occurs in response to a perceived harmful event or threat to survival.

Since then two other responses have been added to the mix, freeze and fix.

Control is established through the application of the four Fs, fight, flight, freeze and fix.

The fight response is an aggressive attempt to control a situation. A person competes at every opportunity and will fight tooth and nail to protect their core values. All situations end in win or lose.

These people behave aggressively to avoid relationships for fear of abandonment or pain.

When a person feels that they are out of their depths and their brain goes into hyper drive, they will take flight from the conflict.

They avoid relationships out of fear of rejection by spending time doing other activities to fill their time.

Freezing is simply to play dead in the face of danger and hope that the threat passes by. This group will avoid social events and spend time on their own.

Fixing is a supplicating approach where the person will do or say anything to remove the conflict as quickly as possible instead of handling the situation in an adult manner.

They also go out of their way to help others, often without being asked, but fail to develop any emotionally ties and connections with the people they help.

An anxious person is permanently cycling in 4F mode. They do not want to be rejected or abandoned to avoid reawakening distressful feelings they experienced in their childhood.

Any external stimulus that directly or indirectly affects their self-confidence or self-esteem levels will trigger an instinctive 4F response.

Therefore, people with anxiety and depression are not bad, they are simply people who have had the complex adult life thrusted upon them at a time they were teenagers.

They looked out to the world through teenage eyes and formed mental rules based on what they experienced at the time and apply the same rules to adult life.

The techniques in this book - will attempt to establish a system that offers a practical set of simple techniques to assist an anxious person to reformat their thought patterns to adult life.

4

I was in a bad way and ready to surrender. What I did next changed my life.

Diagnosed with acute anxiety and depression left me devastated. My family doctor laid out all the available treatments namely cognitive behavioural therapy, support groups, psychiatrists, self-help books and anti-depressants among others.

I was in shock. I never thought that I had anxiety and depression, I simply thought that it was who I was. My personality. My view of how I relate to the world.

This was quite a shock for me at the time, and since I tend to 'leave out if in doubt', I requested for time to learn about the condition before deciding on how to proceed with treatment.
So, I thought the best way to investigate the issue would be to take a thesis approach and formulate a set of question parameters to form a general view of the subject.

As a former print and electronic journalist, I decided to answer the 5Ws and 1H –Who, What, Why, When, Where and How—related to my problem. I have no formal medical or psychiatric qualifications, yet that did not stop me. If I had to learn from scratch, then it is worth putting in the effort.

What is anxiety and depression?
Why does a person become anxious and depressed?
How does a person become anxious and depressed?
How to reverse engineer the problem to identify the source of the anxiety and depression?
How to change the source of anxiety and depression?
Along with a mental approach is there a physical dimension involved?
Is there a method to overcome anxiety without resorting to medical treatment?

At the time, I had no idea of what I was looking for nor what I would find, but I was certain that if I focused on the above questions an idea will form and become the main focal point of my investigative research.

I began reading widely on the subject starting with A level psychology and progressing to degree level books.
I researched sector specific journals, articles by industry experts and acclaimed authors, and watched YouTube videos and motivational speeches related to anxiety and depression.

To support my research I covered subjects on neuro-linguistic programming, behavioural sciences, marketing and sales, meditation, public relations, and the human biological and emotional connection.

I must confess that the research was labour intensive.
As you can imagine, medical terms can be quite complex remember and the reading can be heavy going.
I had to flick through the dictionary at every sentence, used a six-foot whiteboard to draw diagrams, and spend hours identifying trends, patterns and exceptions.
It was a very humbling experience. It made me defensive and angry, but the explanations were too powerful to ignore.
I felt that since my current thinking was the cause of my anxiety and depression, then to get out of it I had to completely change what I would normally do. I realised that I had to surrender to the reading material.

It was emotionally difficult to recognise and accept that certain beliefs that I held were the reasons causing the anxiety and depression.
I had to face up to the fact that I was permanently in 4F mode and never really used my thought processes in an adult manner. Eventually, after years of research, I felt that I had sufficient information to re-wire my thought process.

I practiced a lot of the techniques in this thesis and real progress began to take shape.
Even though I can recognise my anxious behaviours, I spend far too much time self-examining and less time developing meaningful relationships and working to a desired goal.

The research gave me a footing to explain and recognise when I behaved anxiously.
This was not what I had set out to achieve. The challenge was to find a way to flip the balance and overcome it.

5

I had to figure out if I could do this: Finding a process to shift the balance.

My parameters gave me a theoretical overview, but I lacked a practical approach to allow me to cross over the divide and develop relationships and progress in life.

My research directed me to renowned psychoanalyst, Carl Jung, and his theory of archetypes formed a strong basis for my road to recovery. He described the functions of the archetypes, but to make them work for people with anxiety, depression and fear was another story.
My gut instinct recognised a connection somewhere, and I had to establish what it was.
Finding a connection was my only goal, and this manual will show you how I went about doing it.

The medical and scientific community may find my approach and ideas to be oversimplified for such a complex topic, and yet therein lies its beauty.
What makes this manual unique is that it dispenses with complex jargon and conceptually heavy theories. It's been stripped to a working level, but in no shape or form am I declaring that it is a solution to the problem.
The only reason why my thesis is available to you is because I thought that it may be of value to another person, and wanted to play my part in helping the wider community.

6

The limited mind-set that keeps you from getting started.

Are anxiety and depression sufferers really stuck in the past by stubbornly relying on outdated thinking to solve new situations?

According to psychoanalysts, people develop beliefs and behaviours in their teenage years and apply their experiences and thoughts to adult situations.

We developed those beliefs to protect us at a time when we were young, powerless, and immature and our behaviours are influenced by the way our parents and the adults we trusted treated us.

Below is a list of statements from the book Dr Robert Glover. (2003) No More Mr. Nice Guy. Running Press. USA.

His list of behaviours may sound familiar to you as they apply to both men and women:

- I follow the rules, despite my own feelings.
- Obey parents, teachers, and adults without question.
- It is a virtue to put others first, because they will like me.
- I treat others as I would like to be treated.
- If provoked, I must turn the other cheek, because it is the mature thing to do.
- I do not cause any trouble, as I want to avoid worrying my parents.

- I won't take risks because I will be scolded, criticised, and shunned.
- If I make a mistake no matter how innocent, I must hide it, or I will get into trouble.
- We are always told to be careful, avoid risks and look out for the boogieman because we will be harmed.

At first glance, the above behaviours are completely innocent and does reflect a sense of logic, however, all these statements carry a darker side to it.

Without realising, there are so many rules that guide your thinking process and behaviours that eventually conflict with one another and does not work in an adult environment.
These behaviours were ingrained in us as a child and we haven't updated these behaviours to reflect new times and situations.

Remember the smart phone application update example I gave earlier?

7

The best kept secret that you don't even realise or been told about

Below is a list of statements formulated by Dr Robert Glover in his book No More Mr Nice Guy. (Reproduced with permission from the author).

How many of these have you heard of and do any apply to you?

In your current life as an adult, do you find yourself thinking and behaving in the following ways?

1. *You are a giver: You believe that giving is a sign of how good you are and will make people love and appreciate you in return.*
2. *You fix: If a person has a problem, has a need, is angry, depressed or sad, you will frequently attempt to solve or fix the situation (usually without being asked).*
3. *You seek approval from others: Everything you say or do is at some level calculated to gain someone's approval or avoid disapproval.*
4. *You avoid conflict: You seek to keep your world smooth. You avoid doing things that might rock the boat or upset anyone.*
5. *You believe they you must hide any perceived flaws and mistakes. You are afraid that others will get upset with you,*

shame you, or even leave if some mistake or shortcoming is exposed.

6. *You seek the right way to do things: You believe that there is a key to having a happy, problem-free life.*

7. *You repress your feelings: You tend to analyse rather than feel. You may see feelings as a waste of time and energy. You often try to keep your feelings on an even keel.*

8. *You often try to be different from what you believe to be an unfair parent.*

9. *You have difficulty making your needs a priority. You often feel that it is selfish to put your needs first.*

10. *You believe that it is a virtue to put the needs of others before yourself.*

11. *You often make your partner your emotional centre. You are happy when your partner is happy, and sad when they are, thus putting tremendous mental energy in your intimate relationships.*

12. *You are dishonest: You hide your mistakes, avoid conflict, say what you think other people want to hear, and repress your own feelings.*

13. *You are secretive: Because you are so driven to seek approval, you will hide anything that you believe might upset anyone. 'If at first you don't succeed, then hide the evidence'.*

14. *You compartmentalise: You are adept at harmonising contradictory pieces of information about yourself by separating them into individual compartments in your mind.*

15. *You are manipulative: You have a hard time making your needs a priority and have difficulty asking for what you want in clear and direct ways. Thus, creating a sense of powerlessness, and are compelled to resort to manipulation and artifice to meet your own needs.*

16. *You are controlling: A major priority for you is to keep your world smooth, and this creates a need to control events, people around you, and pre-empt any event that may destabilise your life in the future.*

17. *You give to get: Though you tend to be generous givers; your giving often has unconscious and unspoken strings attached. You want to be appreciated, you want reciprocation, you want someone to stop being angry at you etc.*
18. *You often feel frustrated or resentful because of giving so much while seemingly getting so little in return.*
19. *You are passive aggressive: You tend to express your frustration and resentment in indirect, roundabout, and not so nice ways. This includes being unavailable, forgetting, being late, not following through etc.*
20. *You are full of rage: A lifetime of frustration and resentment creates a pressure cooker of repressed rage deep inside you. This erupts at unexpected and inappropriate times.*
21. *You tend to swing back and forth between nice and not so nice.*
22. *You are addictive: The addictive behaviour serves the purpose of relieving stress, altering moods, or medicating pain.*
23. *You have difficulty setting boundaries: Many have a hard time saying NO, STOP, or I'm not going to.*
24. *You often feel like a helpless victim and see the other person as the cause of the problems you are experiencing.*
25. *You are frequently isolated: Though you desire to be liked and loved, your behaviour makes it difficult for people to get very close to you.*
26. *You are attracted to people and situations that need fixing: Because of childhood survival mechanisms, you need to look good on the outside, seek approval and spend much time putting out fires and managing crisis.*
27. *You have problems in intimate relationships: You are a terrible listener because you are too busy trying to figure out how to defend yourself or fix the other person's problem.*
28. *You form relationships with whom you believe are projects and diamonds in the rough.*
29. *Because of your fear of conflict, you are frequently dishonest and are rarely available to work all the way through a problem.*

30. *You are relatively successful: Almost without exception they fail to live up to their potential.*
31. *You tend to be black and white in your thinking.*

After reading his book, I recognised almost every listed trait in me, and I was completely overwhelmed by what I learned. How many do you relate to?

First, I was shocked that Dr Robert Glover hit the nail on every single behaviour I had, and secondly, relieved that I was not the only one with the traits listed.

He explains that parenting skills have changed over time, and it is this nurturing that has led us to develop anxious thought patterns that he calls childhood paradigms.

To learn more about childhood paradigms, I also read Susan Forward with Craig Buck. (2002) Toxic parents. Bantam.
She argues that despite their best intentions, parents have not been able to support a child's growth in a healthy manner.

Her ideas supported many of the arguments made by Dr Glover, and helped me to understand why and how I became entrenched in childhood thinking.

Their research and findings enabled me to identify which parts of my mental software was outdated and what could be the root cause of my anxiety and depression.

How to let go of childhood paradigms became my next step.

I realised that I was slave to the 4Fs and in perpetual defence mode. So I directed my research at how to think before I act instead of reacting out of fear.

The concept of being pro-active in a psychological sense was my goal. When we detect an external stimulus, our brain interprets these signals, and formulates an appropriate response. This is being proactive.

A reactive mind would be to simply react according to the 4Fs.

I found Dr Robert Glover four step technique to avoid the 4Fs very useful.

A person must: Observe, Differentiate, Self-Soothe and emotional detachment, and not Defend, Explain, Excuse and Rationalise (DEER).

In a nutshell, he explains that a person must observe whether they are thinking in a reactive manner.

They must think whether they are behaving in 4Fs, if so then take time to think more before deciding on your desired outcome.

Once you make the decision, allow yourself to become comfortable to the idea that this is the best course of action to take.

Once the decision is being executed, avoid becoming emotionally dependent on the outcome.

Thinking proactively can be tricky at first, as just like I did, you will second guess every thought and action that you make.

Dr Glover recommends running these two questions through your mind:

1. You have to ask yourself: "By thinking or doing this, is it a reactive action or is it something that I have thought through? Am I being reactive, or proactive?"
2. Am I in DEER mode: Defend, Explain. Excuse. Rationalise.

In other words, am I defending my view? Do I feel the urge to justify my actions? Can I find an excuse to justify my actions so that I can feel better? Am I rationalising my act to suit my purpose?

At first, this will be mentally taxing, but after a while it begins to become second nature, and this is the first step on your journey to retrain your mind.

According to Dr Robert Glover, the process for breaking free from childhood paradigms is to accept all good and bad aspects of one's self without guilt or shame.
We must accept that we are who we are and not form any judgements.
He describes this as becoming an 'integrated individual'.

Integrated, is defined as 'with various parts or aspects linked or coordinated', and Dr Glover argues that 'an integrated person embraces the various parts that makes them unique, their personal power, assertiveness, courage, passion as well as their imperfections, mistakes and darker side'.

An integrated person doesn't strive to be perfect or gain the approval of others.
Instead they accept what is 'good enough', or 'what does the job', and accept themselves for who they are.

Dr Glover says that we must *eliminate our childhood paradigms and begin to update our mental software* with the characteristics of an integrated person:

1. *You must have a strong sense of self and like yourself just as you are.*
2. *You take responsibility for meeting your own needs.*
3. *You have integrity and do what is right and not what is expedient.*
4. *You are a leader and willing to provide for and protect those you care about.*
5. *You are clear, direct, and expressive of your feelings.*
6. *You can be nurturing and giving without caretaking or problem solving.*
7. *You know how to set healthy boundaries and is not afraid to work through conflict.*

He explains that a person must learn to *disassociate* from their childhood paradigms and 4Fs traits and replace them with integrated behaviours.

Learning to disassociate

Fear is a normal emotion that serves to alert us to situations that requires our attention and time. Once the task is complete, the fear dissipates, and we move to the next task.
However, for those with anxiety and depression, fear is instead a constant and dominating force.

Psychologist Gerald Rosen in his book, 'Don't be afraid, a program for overcoming fear and phobias', mentions creating new perspectives by mentally distancing yourself from your feelings and take on the perspective of an observer. To disassociate.

He explains how depressed people disassociate from their positive experiences and associate into the negative ones. This makes sense as to why people seem to only see problems, lack clarity of thought and tend to retreat from the world.
Depressed people find that their 4F reactions limits their creativity and thinking when they need it most. Their mind becomes closed to new developments and positive opportunities.

When experiencing grief, the weakness of the Lover quadrant (quadrants are explained later in this thesis), a person disassociates from pleasant memories and associates themselves with the feeling of grief and becoming passive.

Neuro-linguistic programming (NLP) developer Robert Dilt, defines excellence as *'the passionate commitment to something from a self-position'*.

Wisdom is the ability to consciously move back and forth between the self-position and observer position, or in other words a person must learn the ability to switch between association and dis-association.

Dr Glover explained a technique to disassociate from feelings and I supported it with neuro-linguistic programming techniques from the book: Steve Andreas and Charles Faulkner. (2009) The new technology of achievement. William Morrow & Co.

With varying degree of success, I managed to disassociate to some extent to external events and mental states.
I looked for any anxious responses and paid close attention to the thoughts going through my mind.
With pen and paper, I wrote down all my thoughts and put them down under each of the 4F headings.

I had to self-reflect and complete ignore everything happening around me.
I asked: How does this situation make me feel and am I using a four F response here?
OBSE: Is it fight (anger), flight (fear and powerless), or fix (fear, anxious, powerless)?

Or am I going into a victim (powerless) mode where I defend then explain my actions, cook up a self-serving excuse and then rationalise my conclusion to justify my behaviour? (DEER)

This was hard at first, but it became easier the more I practiced. With Dr Glover's advice, it became easier to understand how I felt by a situation and enabled me to identify which of the 4Fs I was exhibiting.

It wasn't easy, but I had somewhat made some headway to consciously make a distinction between a reactive and pro-active action.
I knew what a reactive action was, but I had no idea at the time of what a pro-active thought looked like?

Figuring out a pro-active outcome was very hard. I had no frame of reference.
Each time I thought of an outcome, I had to double check to ensure that it was neither a childhood paradigm trait nor a 4F behaviour.

I spent most of my life living in fear and reacting, that I had no idea of what would make me truly happy. This thought sent chills down my spine.

 The best kept secret that you don't even realise or been told about

The answer came from Steve Andreas and Charles Faulkner. (2009) The new technology of achievement. William Morrow & Co.

I needed a goal that would provide a framework for me to focus my mind on pro-active thoughts and actions. It made sense that pro-active thinking required a specific and clearly defined goal.
When you act in a goal-oriented manner you see signs of progress towards the realisation of the goal, this will no doubt boost your self-worth, self-esteem and self-confidence.

On comparing the situation without a goal, I realised that my actions would be aimless and less rewarding. Sending my self-esteem, self-worth and self-confidence into the opposite direction.

I then assumed that to reduce anxiety and depression, I needed goals that would help boost my self-esteem, self-worth and self-confidence.

Building self-confidence, self-worth and self-esteem

So, what did I have to do to repair my rock bottom self-esteem, bruised self-confidence and low self-worth?

I was in the habit of severely self-criticising and placing unreasonable demands on myself. My mind constantly show-reeled either images of failing or hearing an internal voice telling me that I was useless and not worth success.

To overcome this, I used NLP, as it offers a good technique to learn how to visualise new behaviours and mental habits.
We must learn to make the distinction between *Expectation versus hope.*

In Steve Andreas and Charles Faulkner. (2009) The new technology of achievement.

William Morrow & Co, they explain that expectation generates one mental picture.

The image feels real, bright, colourful, near and you become associated.
This generates greater confidence in any situation.

Hope brings two pictures and introduces some uncertainty. It may or may not happen.
The image is fuzzy, distorted, distant and you become disassociated.
It is the uncertainty that makes us worry and start to focus on problems. Therefore, we must focus on expecting rather than hoping.

For example:
I expect it to be sunny tomorrow, is not the same as, I hope it is sunny tomorrow.

Steps to boost self-appreciation and self-esteem

Self-esteem: An objective and favourable impression of one's self that influences all of one's expectations.
It is the bottom line for peace of mind and personal satisfaction.
Change your internal representation (form and content) of yourself.
SIMPLY THINK of a visually strong image.

Change the way you view a situation

Think of something you like.
Make the image large, colourful, and bright and near, it will raise your self-esteem by bringing positive content.

If you do the opposite, then your self-esteem will plummet. The content that follows will be negative.
Try doing the same exercise, but this time think of something you dislike. Did you feel a difference?

Healthy self-esteeming people are simply aware that their emotions provide deeply important information about how they're living their lives.

They do not associate with the feelings that comes from it. It's only an indicator that certain actions must be taken to achieve what they want.

Think of your emotions as feedback that gives you the opportunity to change your life and how you view yourself.

Distinguish yourself from Being V Doing

John Bradshaw in his book, 'Healing the shame that binds you' purports the idea that:
'You are a human being, not a human doing. You are a human being, not a human performance'.

Learn to separate who you are from what you do. Your behaviour is simply a measuring device that tells you how effective or ineffective you are operating.

Knowing that you are not your behaviour avoids many troubling emotions like regret, self-blame, and shame. This allows all your energy to examine how you are living and to change behaviours and responses that you are not satisfied with.

Self-esteem

With self-esteem you feel safe with yourself, and can say yes or no to people and situations. This gives you freedom of choice without obligation.

'I' statements make you take ownership of your own experiences, wants and needs,
Make bold 'I' statements to empower you to stand up for your ideology, as well as to know and feel the way you want.
I am myself, I am this person, and no one else. I love myself, imperfections and all.

Whereas being compelled to saying 'yes' all the time, leads to low self-esteem.
Lack of choice is often a characteristic of co-dependency and other negative addictive or compulsive behaviours.

Feeling worthless leads to less choices and this is repeated continually on a loop.
Ineffective behaviours lead to fewer success leading to increasing feelings of worthlessness.

As you can see, this turns into a never ending vicious circle of low self-esteem.

Fear of criticism

People with low self-esteem will react defensively if someone was to find fault with their performance, values or goals.

They will feel hurt and helpless if criticised, or respond aggressively to maintain and safeguard their self-esteem.
They are unable to appreciate and accept that everyone has their own unique perspective and model of the world.
They cannot objectively compare another person's opinion to their own.

Healthy mature people with high self-esteem feel good about themselves and in the same situation would be empowered to listen to and to evaluate the accuracy of the other persons point of view, by stepping into the shoes of that person. They use empathy.
They will not feel compelled to accept or reject the others perspective.

If they felt abused they would feel comfortable saying so, and take appropriate action to create a win-win solution wherever possible.

Self-confidence

With a vision in mind, specific outcomes in life will act as milestones that you will recognise as deliberate progress. These indicators will accumulate, and you start to foster confidence in your decision-making abilities.

By taking a decision to meet a vision oriented outcome, it is easier to manage your expectations (Not hope), and become comfortable with the outcome associated with it.

However, without a goal, and no clear vision, you will be at the mercy of the randomness of life.

Being shifted from pillar to post, you have no idea of what decision to take because you don't know where to go, other than a 4F reaction.

It's vital that you try and use every situation or at least parts of a situation to help build your goal.

If not, you will to speculate wildly about what is going to happen next and pray that nothing bad happens. This is fear.

An important lesson needs to be learned here. Not only are vision oriented decisions vital for success, but there is also the need to take a decision and be comfortable with it regardless of the outcome.

Dr Glover calls this the ability to self-soothe. To be able to calm one's mind and emotions once a decision has been taken.

Anxious people tend to worry about a decision and constantly think the worse until the decision has taken effect. Our childhood paradigms surface here. We need to stop worrying about the opinions and judgements of others, and simply accept the outcome without attached feelings.

At best we can learn some positive character building lessons from the outcome.

I found accepting decisions difficult at first. Logically, I agreed that once the wheels of a decision were in motion, I could not influence the outcome. So, I plucked up the courage and took a view that I will deal with any outcome. What's the worst that could happen?

At this point I realised that dealing with fear was another issue I had to tackle.

I was anxious and depressed because of fear. I didn't trust myself enough to be capable to deal with the complexities of the world.

The reading so far allowed me to make certain assumptions, however I needed to consult other disciplines for help on dealing with the fear of fear.

So, am I a product of fear? Were my traits and behaviours a product of my fears?
If an anxious person's mind is consumed with fear, then I had to understand why fear had such a grip on me and its origins. And, what to replace this fear with? There must be something that drove me into this fearful spiral, what was it?

8

Your parents lovingly ruined you by doing this when you were a kid.

Fear is a natural and healthy emotion generated by our mind to keep us alert to any potential or perceived trouble.

Motivational speaker Les Brown describes fear as False Evidence Appearing Real (FEAR).
Thanks to the book by Susan Jeffers. (2007) Feel the fear and do it anyway. Vermilion London, I understood fear and what fearful behaviours were and was able to prevent it from taking my mind completely hostage.

At the time I thought that if I was capable to handle how my fear interferes with my state of mind, then similarly I would be able to avoid being anxious and depressed.

A mature mind uses fear as an indicator and concentrates the mind on unfolding events. The brain recognises that an action will be required and therefore prepares itself to respond in line with your goals.
Anxious minds associate fear with hurt and pain, and instinctively try to fix and control a situation.
These fears play out in our minds, and to deal with them, we develop coping mechanisms to protect ourselves.
One of our coping mechanisms is to close out the world around us.

According to Susan Jeffers at the bottom of every one of our fears is that we don't trust ourselves to handle whatever life may throw at us.

I found this an interesting concept, as this was never an idea I held about myself.
At the time I struggled with the idea but after thinking about it, and by drawing ideas from the research, I realised that she had a point.

All you need to do to lessen your fear is to trust your ability to handle whatever comes your way.
Every time you feel afraid, remind yourself that it is simply because you are not feeling good enough about yourself and uncertain of the outcome. You cannot control the outcome so there is no point wasting energy thinking about it. Focus your energy on other goals instead.

Why do we have little trust in ourselves? This stems back to our childhood, and the mental thought patterns developed at that age.
In her book, Susan Jeffers explains that parents did their best to protect us, however their nurturing and advice reinforced messages of 'be careful', 'don't take risks, 'I don't want anything to happen to you'.
These words of love and affection were instead mentally internalised as 'you cannot be trusted with your own welfare'.

We hear words like: You won't be able to handle the disappointment, you are not clever enough, you cannot survive without my guidance, you cannot handle the doom and gloom of life, and the cumulative effect over time is severe self-doubt. Susan Forward with Craig Buck. (2002) Toxic parents. Bantam also supports this argument with her findings.

It is lack of trust in yourself that is stopping you from getting what you want out of life.

Can it be really lack of trust that equates to fear?

So, to overcome fear is to believe that you can handle anything. It may be a great decision or not, or it could be a decent one. Who cares, you learn from it and move on to the next goal.

According to Jefferies, we must trust that we have done our best under the circumstances and will accept a positive result instead of a perfect result.

To identify a positive result or one that can be used as a learning experience, ask the following questions and see if you can tick yes:

Have I Considered all the available options?
Am I sufficiently knowledgeable on this subject?
Was the research on the topic deep enough?
Did I have the appropriate tools for the job?

I realised that to overcome fear I had to act pro-actively towards my goals. So, to my mind, any progress towards achieving a goal meant I would become less fearful and more pro-active. There was a dual effect.

It dawned that the real game changer to overcome anxiety and depression was to set myself clear goals, identify the steps to achieve my goals, and use the above techniques to avoid behaving and thinking in an anxious manner.

This was confirmation that my research was developing towards something concrete and useful.

I was satisfied with what I had covered in the psychological part of my research, so I then turned my attention to the physical side of anxiety and depression.

9

Save your time and energy by following this shortcut

Anxiety and depression suppresses dopamine and serotonin production in the body, and I felt that it would be important to learn how to naturally stimulate these two hormones to help me in overcoming anxiety and depression.

Your physical health has a direct impact on the functioning of your mind.
Every heard the saying: a healthy body and a healthy mind? If yes, then what does a healthy body really mean?

We are told to exercise regularly, eat healthily, stay hydrated, take care of any signs of illness, and taking precautionary measures to remain strong and functional for the future.

And yet we do not know how often to exercise, which foods are best, how much water is enough, what are the signs I need to look out for to avoid developing certain health concerns in the future.

Uninterrupted eight-hour sleep is important as the brain releases hormones that relieve cortisol build up in the body, but with a busy lifestyle we tend to sleep less and less. Cortisol is a stress hormone and builds up over time causing untold amounts of harm to the brain and body.

Most of these questions can be answered and addressed by qualified and experienced personal trainers, dieticians, or your family doctor.

You don't necessarily need to go to the gym, as you can also do some fitness routines in your own home for at thirty minutes a day. There is no excuse to put this off to be honest.
Seek professional advice and put in place a physical and dietary health action plan to remain physically and mentally healthy to support you in your quest to become a pro-active person.

As a health professional, I ensured that I consumed a nutritious diet and paid close attention to how I train and the type of macronutrients and micronutrients I ate.
The research indicated that I had to increase my consumption of serotonin and dopamine boosting foods. I learnt that the brain only produced 10% Serotonin, whereas 90% was produced in the gut.
This was quite surprising, and as I dug deeper I came across the vagus nerve and pineal gland and how it taps into serotonin reserves affecting emotions, reducing stress, heart rate and blood pressure.

The vagus nerve changes the functions of certain parts of the brain, stimulates digestion and can be indirectly stimulated to relieve anxiety and depression.
Healthy gut bacteria were essential in keeping the gut healthy, so I increased my intake of fibre and probiotics.

Stimulation of the vagus nerve was the next step in my research. I had to find out about this because from my understanding gut health would be crucial for my recovery.

10

Get emotionally high legally for free anywhere and anytime

If you are expecting something fabulous and out of this world to do this, then you will be disappointed.
I found that the way to stimulate the vagus nerve is through breathing.

When stimulated the vagus nerve releases serotonin into the body and this helps balance out the hormonal side of anxiety and depression.

So, was there something wrong with my breathing?
This was awkward because I paid closer attention and found that I tended to take short and shallow breaths instead of slow and deep breaths.

On YouTube, I found hundreds of professed methods on how to breathe with each method claiming different benefits, so I selected the breathing techniques that were associated with stimulating the vagus nerve.
After countless trials and error, I eventually found a style that was pioneered by Harvard trained Dr Andrew Weill.

He recommends using 4-7-8 second counts. You inhale rapidly for 4 seconds, hold your breath for 7, and then gently exhale for 8 seconds. Interestingly I noticed that I was able to push back the mental noise and achieve a somewhat lightening of the mind.

The more I focused on my breath, I was able to somehow stop my mind from wandering randomly.

This was very encouraging at first, but then without notice, unsolicited thoughts crept back in.
I could only switch off in starts and fits, however the momentary instant of calm made me believe that this was possible.
Where were these thoughts coming from?
Why is it that the more silent my mind becomes, the more noise my mind tries to generate?

What was the relationship between silence and random thoughts?

11

Does this stimulus drive you crazy and why do you keep feeding it?

Do you constantly fill your mind with thoughts and actions?
Do you think that it is bad for your mind to be still and silent?

Spiritual teacher Eckhart Tolle had the answer to my questions and in his YouTube video he explains that silence of the mind is different from being silent.

'Silenceofthemindistheabilitytoswitchoffyourmindsothatitisinneutral. Orinotherwords,bykeepingyourawarenessinaneutralorrelaxedstate. Whereas being silent means not speaking or not making any noises. There is a big difference. It is important to make and appreciate the depth of this distinction'.

When your mind is silent, it allows the mind to rest, enabling it to focus its awareness on important goal oriented tasks when deliberately called into action.
He goes on to add that 'the mind is suited to single tasking, not multi-tasking as it you can only focus your awareness on one thing at a time'.

This was a very telling statement. I originally held the belief that multi-tasking was something that we were all expected to perform and failure to multi-task was frowned upon.

But after hearing his podcast, I understood that mental multi-tasking was making my brain over active, and my brain had become accustomed to this.
This went some way to explain why thoughts kept creeping into my mind whilst I carried out the breathing exercises.

It is fine to multi-task in life, but not to a point where it makes us anxious, depressed, sad, angry and fearful.
Motivational speaker Zig Ziglar often mentions that rather than be a wandering generality, you must learn how to be a meaningful specific.
Perform one thing to completion before tackling the next activity.
This statement by Ziglar tied in with Eckhart's assertion of a single tasking mind.

To overcome anxiety and depression, or even anger, sadness, and fear, it was important to be comfortable with a silent mind and then learn to focus my attention on a single task.

So how did I dampen the noise, and focus my mind to be specific?
Once I appreciated the importance of what I had found from various sources, I set my mind to put into practice all the steps and attempted to quite my mind and become comfortable with silence.
I knew what I need to achieve, and this helped me direct my thoughts.
The noise interfered at first, but I was eventually able to focus on a single task. This seemed to do the trick and I ran with it.

12

Did this occur to you when you tried previous treatments?

Despite quietening the mental chatter during my breathing exercises, I found that negative fearful anxious thoughts kept creeping in.
I felt powerless at the time because I realised that this was holding me back from trying to overcome my anxiety and depression.
Logically I understood that the longer I had been under the influence of anxiety, depression, sadness, grief and anger, the harder and longer will be the process to remove it.

But why was my mind resisting my deliberate attempts to stop negative thoughts from hijacking my mind?
For some reason Newton's third law of motion came to mind.
It states that: Every force experiences an equal and opposite force.

Where there is a force, there is resistance, so I then reasoned that the negative thoughts were surely resistance to my conscious effort to focus on a single task.
The resistance manifesting itself in the form of negative talk, self-doubt, addictions and fear.

We experience resistance every day. The bed covers on your body, the movement of your toothbrush against your teeth, the accumulation of dust on furniture, the pressing down of your finger on a button, and every step you take on a hard surface, all has resistance.

We don't consciously think about these resistance forces when carrying out these daily tasks, we don't even notice it. We simply accept it and act as if it was never there.

I then began looking at the negative chatter in a new way. I knew now that the presence of resistance was normal, and I simply did my best to ignore it when performing breathing exercises.
When you identify negative thoughts as natural resistance, it becomes easier to snap back to your focus on the breathing. You no longer associate the feeling of fear to the thought.
It will never go away, but with constant practice you will learn to push it into the background.

The better you become at calming down the mind the more potent and vicious the resistance will become, accordance of Newton's third law of motion states the bigger the effort, the greater the resistance.

So I changed tactic. An anxious person will aim to stop the negative chatter, and in contrast a mature mind will tone the resistance chatter all the way down.

My next question was how to tone down the chatter. I wrote down all the negative chatter and after a while I noticed that the intensity and length of the chatter varied according to how I felt on the day. This was quite intriguing, so I set out to find out more about the relationship between mood and anxiety and depression.

13

Mind blowing, literally. Why hasn't anyone explained it this way?

This led me to discovering a wealth of material on the impact of emotional states on anxiety and depression. I focused my research on the works of neurologist and founder of psychoanalysis Sigmund Freud, and Psychiatrist and Psychoanalyst Carl Jung.

In light of my research I had a decent grasp of his material, but it was 'King, Warrior, Magician, and Lover: Rediscovering the archetypes of the mature masculine' by Jungian psychologist Robert Moore and mythologist Douglas Gillette that clinched it for me.

It explains that there are four states of mind associated with depression and anxiety.
Dr Robert Moore explains that we all have four gateway emotional states: Joy, Anger, Sadness and Fear.

After examination of the book KWML, I made a summary highlighting the following: it was governed by a weakness, how it is triggered, can it be switched off, what is its main function, and does each archetype interact.

So, I categorised the negative chatter under the four states and realised that Dr Moore may have an explanation as to how I can tone down the negative chatter.

I thought why not see if this works.
If it does, then was there a way to apply KWML to create healthy adult thought patterns and behaviours?

The four quadrants and their respective functions:

King gateway emotion: Anxiety
Weakness: Fear. Afraid to act. Risk averse.
Primary function: Creating a vision and feeling of wellbeing. Passive state.
Action: Once a vision is set, it must take bold and confident action to overcome any fear. It must ignore negative thought processes by moving to a pro-active state.

Warrior gateway emotion: Anger
Weakness: Aggression/anger- Deep sense of something lost/denied/ taken leading to lack of wellbeing.
Primary function: Goal oriented, confident, bold and decisive. Follows a goal without personal sentiment. A sense of duty towards goal. Refining skillset. Active state.
Action: Meet your needs before they run out. Learn to express your anger through mature adult means.

Magician gateway emotion: Sadness
Weakness: sadness. A high confidence in logic without emotional involvement.
Primary function: Practising and executing skills, applying wisdom and connections in the world to achieve your vision.
Be willing to say I don't know and ask for help.
Assess your strengths and weaknesses in the execution of your plans. Seeks wellbeing.
Action: Executing action to meet your needs before they go into shortage by being thoughtful and humble.

Lover gateway emotion: Grief
Weakness: Enjoyment of senses over responsibility.

Primary function: Strong feeling of calm, fulfilment and enjoyment. Expressions of enjoyment.

Action: Learn to take responsibility for your own growth and control your enjoyment. Seek out knowledge, resources and new skills to complete unresolved goals.

I understood the traits of each quadrant, but what I had to investigate was the way they interacted and how to decide which option was best.

This is my interpretation of the diagram and how to go about using it to help decide on a course of action or suppress any signs of anxiety or depression.

Key to the KWML Diagram

1. When applying goal setting follow the diagram in a clockwise direction.
2. When altering current feeling, identify your quadrant and then move to the quadrant which has the feeling you want to be in.
3. When you have completed the process within the quadrant, switch to the next stage of the KWML cycle.
4. Point O=balance, Y= High logical, X= Extreme low esteem, --Y=High emotional joy, --X= Low emotional confidence. Aim is to balance yourself at point O.

Passive state: King and Lover, Well-being quadrants. Imagining a vision.

Active state: Warrior and Magician. Action and logical quadrants. Making vision a reality.

If the mind single tasks, and if NLP follows the order Mission, Goal, Execution and Result, this would confirm that the aim of the KWML diagram was not to remain in separate quadrants and move in a clockwise circle.

But it was to converge towards the middle of all four quadrants, at point O.

Would this mean we could operate at all four levels simultaneously?

Is this the very point that Dr Glover mentioned earlier as being 'integrated'?

Would this also mean that we would be operating with adult maturity?

Y	
King: Sets Vision	Warrior: Sets goals to achieve vision
Gateway emotion: Joy/Fear/Anxiety	Gateway emotion: Anger/Fear
Weakness:	Weakness:
Fear of success/failure and overthinking	Anger/passive aggressive/violent
Afraid to take action and is risk averse	Strength:
Strength;	Logical, goal-oriented, bold and confident.
Well-being, logical, strategic, thoughtful.	Meets goals before essential items are depleted.
Must take bold confident action to meet goal.	
-- X **O**	**X**
Lover: Balances responsibility and enjoyment	Magician: Execution of skills to working on goal.
Gateway emotion: Joy/Grief/Anxiety	Gateway emotion: Sadness
Weakness: Over-enjoyment of senses at the expense of personal and professional responsibilities.	Weakness: High confidence in logical thinking without attaching any emotions.
Strength:	Strength:
Well-being, Strong feeling of calm and enjoyment, nurturing and affectionate.	High emotional confidence/motivated/ hungry.
Reflect and take corrective action by building on experience and learn new skills for continual personal growth and to achieve magician success.	Highly knowledgeable and skilled.
	Meet your needs by applying skills before essentials are in shortage.
--Y	

<u>The king quadrant</u>

The king quadrant is where you formulate your vision, and its worst enemy is over-thinking. So, I felt that vision creation would be important here.
Steve Andreas and Charles Faulkner. (2009) The new technology of achievement. William Morrow & Co. page 79 sets out an easy to follow set of steps for mission creation.

A mission is a sense of purpose that lures you into the future. It unifies your beliefs, values, actions and your sense of who you are. It's a fabric woven of the various threads of your interests, desires, goals.

Once you have your vision, your imagination becomes focused as you now have a purpose.

'If one advances confidently in the direction of their dreams, you will meet with a success unexpected in common hours-Henry David Thoreau'
President JFK: "We choose to go to the moon in this decade and do the things not because they are easy but because they are hard. Because that goal will serve to organise and measure the best of our energies and skills".

What is your purpose?

1. Find your inner excitement and know your passions, desires, and loves. Make a list.
2. Focus on successful people who have been through it already and read their biographies.
    See how they approached and tackled similar situations. Learn as much as you can.
3. Replicate their actions and review your purpose three times a day.

This will make you focus and concentrate. When that negative conversation begins to tell you what you cannot do, your concentration will instead focus on your purpose and mission.

    Mind blowing, literally. Why hasn't anyone explained it this way?

On page 123 in Steve Andreas and Charles Faulkner. (2009) The new technology of achievement. William Morrow & Co, describes a mission as a 'reflection of oneself. It defines how we use our inner abilities and guides how we act in this world. A mission creates meaningful action'.

He puts forward the following steps:

A strong mission must include all your mission stages at the individual, work, personal, and larger than life goals.

Consider:
- I am a sage, with an aim to share knowledge and know-how.
- I am a consultant at work, where I meet peoples' expectations with services that meet their goals.
- I am a man who aims to provide and secure my family and legacy.
- I am an agent of change, who aims to inspire others to live a healthier lifestyle, achieve their goals.

Once you have a vision in mind, you are ready for the next stage. You start to think about setting several actionable mini-goals that will help to serve your mission.

Notice how at this stage you have only been thinking and no physical action is required. This quadrant is for thinking, and now the thinking is over, it becomes idle and looks for something to think about. This is when the negative chatter sneaks in.

Without a vision, overthinking no longer acts an indicator, it has turned into a paralysing force instead.
Each time you think of an idea, you somehow always seem to find something that defeats it. You constantly play out scenarios without ever making any actual real progress as you become risk averse. The ideas keep turning through your mind and you can't make it stop.

Negative chatter is a sign of overthinking. It is an indicator that action is now required to launch in pursuit of your specific goals.

As soon as you become aware of the over-thinking, then you know it is now time to shift from a passive state into an active state, the warrior quadrant.

The warrior quadrant is responsible for establishing mini-goals with desired outcomes.
The idea is that the warrior will acquire the skills and tools necessary to fulfil the mission.
Here you carry out a SWOT/PESTL (Strength, weakness, opportunities, threats, political, economic, social, technological and legal) analysis and then you lay out a set of strategies to accomplish your desired outcomes.

Once your analysis is completed, overthinking will kick in, indicating once again that it is time to move into the next quadrant, i.e. the magician quadrant.

In the magician quadrant, you are expected to execute the strategies laid out in the warrior quadrant.
You use your skills and knowledge to apply in play tactics to keep you on track of your goals.
The tactics could be for example, knowing how to network, knowing how to convey value, understanding how to motivate others among others, making sound decisions, making appropriate choices etc.
In this quadrant, other people are also operating and doing the same thing.
There will be moments when you find yourself competing with someone else for the same desired outcome. Not everyone plays fair. And this is where a childhood paradigm may play against you.
There are no established rules that govern peoples attitude towards fair play. Life is not fair and there is no fairy tale ending, so we must not expect others to treat us fairly.
It is not that they are bad, it is that we must stop thinking with our childhood paradigms.

In the magician quadrant, Game theory and finite v infinite wars are important to understand.

It explains that the world does not abide by natural law. There is no sense of morally right or wrong, nor any sense of good and bad. This is where our childhood paradigms hold us back from succeeding in this quadrant.

The theory explains certain realities, that we as anxiety, depression and fear sufferers never really understood.

Dr Moore warns that after practising the KWML exercises, people around you will notice how your behaviour and attitude will have improved.

Some will congratulate and encourage, but on the other side, your positive outlook will attract people who may manipulate and control your attitude and expectations.

They will try and suck out your positivity. It does not mean that they are bad people, simply it is in their nature and that they are oblivious to it.

It was at this point that I realised that everyone operates in the magician quadrant and here people will fight tooth and nail to achieve their goals.

They may be nice people, but they may not use fair tactics to get what they want.

Initially I thought that when this happened, they were deliberately targeting me, but now I realise that it is simply the competitive nature of being human. If it wasn't me, then someone else would have felt their wrath.

This made me feel better as I knew now that I was not a targeted victim or prey for those around me.

Therefore success will depend on staying clear of these people, and be around people who are visionaries, goal setters, and closers.

When your new mindset cements, even negative people will not be able to knock you off your stride and you may change negative influences into positive by your presence.

In the face of criticism, ask yourself:
"What can I do that will allow me to remain resourceful no matter what criticism comes my way?
Give yourself a self-worth boost by improving the way you look, dress and communicate. People respond when you display strong congruent behaviours. You must equally make good on your promises.

How will you know when you have achieved your goal and time to move into the fourth lover quadrant?
There are three possible outcomes.
You may have completed your mini-goal, the process was still in progress, or it failed.

If you meet your goal then you can move ahead into the lover quadrant as it is associated with joy and well-being.

Even if you fail to meet your goal due to the competitive nature of the quadrant you will notice sadness growing inside you and this is when you phase shift into the Lover quadrant.
If you don't shift, you will spark the 4Fs and engage in trickery by manipulation and controlling behaviour to secure a goal oriented result. So, you must shift at the right time.
To succeed in the magician quadrant, it is important to create rapport and strong relationships. The strength of your network and ability to secure results are crucial.

So, I thought that I needed to perhaps re-train/refresh my people and professional skills.
It is true that working life is competitive, but I hadn't realised that the way I handled the competition was from an anxious place.
This would go a long way to explain why certain events in the past took unexpected turns. I was able to see past experiences in a new light.

I needed to learn how to make people feel comfortable and demonstrate a concern for the values they hold dear. People like to work with people they like and trust, this is rapport.

I used NLP techniques from Steve Andreas and Charles Faulkner. (2009) The new technology of achievement. William Morrow & Co, to determine how to:

1)   Set mutually satisfying goals.
2)   Establish and maintain non-verbal rapport.
3)   Produce positive feelings in others

1.   Mutually satisfying goals

What kind of relationship do you want?

Set goals that involve others. Keep your goals in mind and discover the goals of others, then seek out people with similar goals to achieve them.

Find out where they go on holiday, what they do for fun, what matters to them personally, and send cards, thank you notes, and offer any information that will interest or educate them.

There are many clues in how they dress, things they own, their habits, and the way they treat people.

Ask: "What will be the expected impact of getting this goal both for me and others involved?
What do I want in this relationship that is positive?
What can I do to make this happen?
What will I see hear, feel that will let me know I achieved this?
When, where, whom and in what context do I want this goal?

Listen, learn and discover what people value. This is the single most important aim of persuasion.
Persuasion is the ability to offer compelling value to others. Not yours, but theirs. This is the magician in you.
Persuasive people are those who can see and hear how others express their values and who can ask the questions to discover their core values.

Then they can demonstrate how their product or service will satisfy the persons' values and provide benefits to them.

Persuasion can also be used to motivate others to do achieve their goals by seeking out what is in their best interests.

1.   Simply ask people:

What's important to you about a phone system?
What do you value in an employee?
What does a motivated staff mean for your company?
Think of your best manager. What are the characteristics that make them a good manager and set them apart from ordinary managers?

2.   You could have a pitch like below:

I believe that our product/service is excellent. However, I also know that it is only appropriate for those who want, need and value what this product has to offer.
Some people think of me as a salesperson, but I think of myself as a consultant whose job it is to find out whether there is a good match between your needs and our products.
To do this, I need to know what you want in a (insert the need here).

3.   Next, once you find their needs, discover the material specifications and criteria.
For example: A client needs is a quality car.
Material specification: It must have these specific qualities.
Criteria: Because it will last longer/requires less repair.
The criteria is the higher value.
Identify whether the criteria are motivated towards or away and this will provide an improved basis to sell your product.

4.   What will be securing the higher criteria do for you? Is it motivation towards or away?

Once you determine the motivation direction, align your pitch with motivational direction actions in combination with their criteria.

The way you weave together your pitch is by using the preferred communication channel being used by the other person.

After delivering your pitch, assurance comes next by adding sub-modalities.
Pay attention to body language clues. During the interaction, pay attention to their facial features.

If they are looking up, talking fast with disjoined thoughts then they are accessing their visual abilities.
If they are looking down to Left: What was said, heard or read, touching face, auditory sense.
Looking down to right: Grasp, talking slow, touching body, sense of touch.

Responses could be:
-      I see what you mean.
-      I hear what you are saying.
-      I've got a grasp on what you've laid out.

If they are accessing their feelings, you can say: I've got a grasp on what you've laid out (feelings). There are however certain difficulties (motivation away) but before they get too close and start breathing down your neck (sub-modalities), let me explain how I can offer some relief (feelings from pain that feeds their motivation away).

Close the conversation with the following outcomes:
If the motivational direction is towards: This product will provide so and so benefits.
If the motivational direction is away: This product will not give you such and such problems.

The more important you elicit the criteria the more value it will have. The higher the value you satisfy, the more persuasive you will become.

Remember that the success of your Warrior goals, will depend on the quality of cooperation from others.
Your mantra must be:
"You are in the business of building relationships through offering value and entertainment with your product and quality of service."

2.   Establish and maintain non-verbal rapport

Finding ways to be alike reduces our differences and we find common ground to build relationships. Develop a loss of rapport detection alarm. As you move out of sync, a feeling of discomfort will emerge, and this will alert you to make a course correction.

All the while, pay attention to personal congruence.
You must be in total alignment during the engagement and give the person your undivided attention. Display excitement, enthusiasm, charisma, and personal power.

To re-establish rapport, you must match their body language, mirror their voice patterns, and harmonise with their overall tempo. Be subtle and do it gradually without the other person noticing.

3.   Produce positive feelings in others.

You must show your competence by setting/defining clear, direct and well-formed goals.
Non-verbal behaviour must be congruent with verbal behaviour.
Be associated with feeling good and deliver the goods on what you are proposing.

Once you have reached the end of your goal, your outcome will be either success or failure and this is when you move into the Lover quadrant.

     Mind blowing, literally. Why hasn't anyone explained it this way?

If you are successful you reward yourself in proportion with the value you place on the achievement and move to the warrior quadrant.

Prioritise your goals depending on the circumstances and resources at your disposal.
Select a goal, then go through the quadrants. After each completion of a goal, then move to the second prioritised goal and so on. Eventually your vision will begin to take shape.

If you are unsuccessful you do not reward yourself, but go straight to the warrior quadrant and use lessons learned through the process to have another crack at the failed mission.
In the warrior quadrant you must work in developing the skills and resources that you lacked in the first attempt.

The NLP techniques will help you stay on track.
I thought that my goal would be complete once I use goal setting and how it influenced anxiety and depression.

But through the works of Carl Jung, and my personal experience, I found that my goals and ideas were directly influenced by the way I felt at the time.
Surely being in a positive mood would mean positive goals and this made me think about my earlier question as to 'pushing the negative chatter into the background'.

How to influence my mood was my next step.

Now I needed to learn about the emotional part of the mind.

Emotional state and the state of mind

In KWML, Dr Robert Moore explains that each archetype displays a specific emotion and that the aim was to put these emotions in balance, and earlier we also found that the mind requires a goal to act pro-actively.

Based on this, an assumption can be made that since an anxious mind has no goal to aim for, it would leave the person in a state of perpetual mood swings ranging from joy, anger, sadness and fear.

So, to avoid feeling a way, it would be sufficient to recognise the feeling and then move into the quadrant with the corresponding positive feeling that you would like to experience.

I found that the King and Lover quadrant was associated with well-being and therefore I knew that I had to be in these quadrants to uplift my emotion or mood.
To change my feelings I had to adopt the quadrant's traits.

My aim was to use the matrix and attempt to put together a process that would assist me in finding balance.

Based from what I had learned so far, I assumed that the inner mind followed the circular pattern KWML. I also applied the concept that the mind can only single task and that the mind requires a goal to remain pro-active.
I assumed that I should focus on a single goal and only begin to tackle other goals once the first goal was completed.

The opposite would be true for anxious minds. The mind in this case does not follow the KWML circular pattern.

The mind pattern is distorted with our feelings randomly fluctuating within the quadrants.
Anxious, depressed and fearful mind patterns do not follow the order KWML, instead it is randomised like LMKW, WKML, LWKM. No wonder anxious people feel the way they do.

This explains why the traditional material on anxiety and depression did not work. This explains why people have difficulty in understanding motivational tapes, cognitive behavioural therapy, anti-depressants, mindfulness and positive thinking.

   Mind blowing, literally. Why hasn't anyone explained it this way?

I realised that this was why my previous attempts at recovery were constantly thwarted. My anxious mind was making me more anxious.

The METHOD A

KWML Diagram

<table>
<tr><td>

King: Sets Vision
Gateway emotion: Joy/Fear/Anxiety

Weakness:
Fear of success/failure and overthinking
Afraid to take action and is risk averse.
Low-self-worth and self-esteem.
Strength:
Well-being, logical, strategic, thoughtful.

Must take bold confident action to meet goal.

</td><td>

Warrior: Sets goals to achieve vision
Gateway emotion: Anger/Fear

Weakness:
Anger/passive aggressive/violent

Strength:
Logical, goal-oriented, bold and confident.

Meets goals before essential items are depleted.

</td></tr>
<tr><td>

Lover: Balances responsibility and enjoyment

Gateway emotion: Joy/Grief/Anxiety

Weakness: Over-enjoyment of senses at the expense of personal and professional responsibilities. Low self-esteem/self-worth.

Strength:
Well-being, Strong feeling of calm and enjoyment, nurturing and affectionate.

Reflect and take corrective action by building on experience and learn new skills for continual personal growth and to achieve magician success.

</td><td>

Magician:

Gateway emotion: Sadness

Weakness: High confidence in logical thinking without attaching any emotions.

Strength:
High emotional confidence/motivated/hungry.
Highly knowledgeable and skilled.

Meet your needs by applying skills before essentials are in shortage.

</td></tr>
</table>

The diagram is arranged with **Y** at the top, **O** and **X** at the centre, with **-- X** at the left-centre, **X** at the right, and **--Y** at the bottom-left.

Based on what I understood and by applying my assumptions, I found that to use the KWML chart to overcome anxiety and depression was as follows:

Steps to overcome anxiety, depression and fear, or boost core values.

Identify which emotion you want to avoid now?
To overcome anxiety/fear: Move into and adopt traits in Magician/Lover quadrants
To overcome grief/sadness: Move into and adopt traits of King/Warrior quadrants

Or

Identify which core values you want to boost now, self-esteem, self-confidence, or self-worth?
To seek self-worth and self-esteem: Move and adopt traits in King/Lover quadrants
To seek confidence: Move and adopt traits in Warrior/Magician quadrants

Instructions on how to use the MATRIX:

1)   (1) Identify how you are feeling at any moment? Anxious, anger, sadness or grief.
OR
(2) Identify if you lack self-esteem, self-worth, or self-confidence.

2)   (1) That emotion is linked to either the KW/ML quadrants. Each archetype has its own characteristics so move into the quadrant that best describes your current emotional state.
OR
(2) If you lack self-esteem and self-worth, then you will be linked to the Lover/King quadrant.
If you lack self-esteem, and sad or angry, you are in the Lover or King quadrants.
If you lack self-esteem and anxious or in grief, you are in the King or Lover quadrant.

       Mind blowing, literally. Why hasn't anyone explained it this way?

If you lack self-worth and sad, you are in the Lover quadrant.
If you lack self-worth and angry or anxious, you are in the King quadrant.
If you are low in confidence and also angry, you are in the Warrior quadrant.
If you are low in confidence and sad about your situation then you are in the magician quadrant.

These will be your starting points. If there is an overlap of quadrants, treat each emotion or core value separately. Make a list of priorities.

3)   Now identify the quadrant where you would like to be.
(1) For example, if feeling fear/anxious then move from KW into your Magician/Lover quadrants.
The idea here is to step out of the KW frame of mind, and use the Magician characteristics to look at the situation and establish if your efforts are working well.
If your efforts are paying off and serving to meet your warrior goals in line with your Kings vision, then you will feel a sense of well-being when you move to the Lover quadrant. This quadrant will provide a sense of re-assurance replacing the feeling of anxiety and fear.

If you feel grief or sadness, then move from Lover/Magician quadrants to the King/Warrior quadrants respectively.
If you are feeling grief, then this is because you did not succeed in completing your goal.
You feel like you have failed and wallow in self-pity. Instead you must identify what went wrong, and make adjustments in the Warrior quadrant.
You must immediately move into the Warrior quadrant and start again before the grief takes root.
When sadness overcomes you, it is time to move towards the King quadrant and remind yourself why you are doing what you are doing. This will inspire you to carry on in realising your vision.
OR

(2) If you are in the Warrior quadrant, you must move into the Lover quadrant and see how you would celebrate completing the goal. Set a compelling reward that would be in proportion to the size of the achievement. This will boost your self-esteem and self-worth.

If in the Magician quadrant, then move into the King quadrant and feel the sense of achievement once the hard work has been completed. Visualise the difference it will make and its impact once the vision is achieved. This will boost your self-confidence.

4) Now that you have moved to the desired quadrant, pay attention to whether the quadrant is passive or active.

(1) If step 3 lands you in the WM quadrant then you must be active to meet your goal. This means that some action on your behalf is required.

But if you are in a KL quadrant then you are in a passive state and must think about how to move towards your goal. This is a time for contemplation only. Either to review your vision, or perhaps review what went wrong with the execution in the Magician quadrant.

OR

(2) If to boost core values, you find yourself in the Warrior or Magician quadrant, then you must take actions that will boost your confidence and self-worth. Invest in a treat that will get your pulses and blood pumping through your system.

If you are in the King or Lover quadrant, you must boost your self-esteem and self-worth by believing that you deserve to achieve your vision and reap the rewards in relation to your effort and the level of complexity you applied.

Treat yourself to an activity that similarly resembles something that you aspire to have one day. For example, an expensive suit or a business class trip. Just to get a feel what life would be like.

5) For all quadrants, the aim is to move your inner mind to be in the centre of all four archetypes at the same time at Point O.

Here you can display all four archetypes at once and be in balance, emotionally and also in terms of establishing high self-esteem, self-confidence, and self-worth.

   Mind blowing, literally. Why hasn't anyone explained it this way?

Operating at all four levels at once would remove any anxiety, depression and fear, and also boost all the core values.

I now had a deeper understanding of how the KWML matrix operated. However, I had to verify that it worked and would work in most situations. So, I went back to listening to motivational videos and applied what I had learned.

14

Affirmations are boring. Try this instead.
It's a lot more fun.

Have you listened to motivational videos and despite the words of empowerment and encouragement it has no lasting effect on you? Have you given their advice a go and despite your efforts you feel no different? I also had the same experience.

My anxious mind couldn't connect with the motivational speeches because they were not formatted to follow the KWML pattern nor was my mind centred.

Armed with what I gathered, and by applying the KWML steps above, I listened to the tapes again.
I realised that motivational speakers didn't arrange their speeches based on the KWML pattern.
I re-arranged the speeches in a KWML order, and surprisingly I understood the tapes in a wholly different way. New messages emerged, and new thoughts came to mind.

My advice would be for you to find a preferred motivator and re-arrange their messages in the KWML pattern.
Revisit any past motivational material and apply the KWML format, Vision, Goal, Execution, Result.
Motivational speeches will begin to make better sense.

15

Let's see if we can try this together right now with a quick result.

Our goal is to overcome our anxiety and depression.

From our earlier work, we found out what were our childhood paradigms and 4F responses.
Now we know what to avoid, we go to the:

King quadrant sets a vision: To become a healthy mature adult free of anxiety and depression.

Warrior quadrant will set mini-goals:
- Improve my physical health with exercise and diet.
- Remove all anxious behaviours by using disassociation techniques.
- Learn how to set goals.
- Identify and develop the skills and tools required to achieve my mini-missions.
- Learn how to breathe when faced with distractions or resistance.

The tools I have are: Preventive healthcare professional, mind exercises, develop self-mastery of my skills, and researching.

Magician will execute the task:
Regularly check that my actions and efforts are all geared towards meeting my goals and working towards my vision.

If it isn't then make a course correction and use new tactics.
Lover: Does this outcome feel right to me?
If yes, then appreciate your headway and move to the warrior quadrant and start a new goal.
If not, then I must re-assess my in-field tactics, and upskill my weaker areas that caused the failure or failures in the magician quadrant.

Now I move back to the warrior quadrant and add new instruments/tools/skills identified in the Lover quadrant and execute my efforts again in the Magician quadrant.
Repeat the process until you succeed in meeting your goal.

However, REMEMBER, life is dynamic, so you must also constantly assess whether your priority order list requires re-ordering.
Maybe today, your priorities are all in order, but a change in circumstances may require you to re-shuffle the pack.

The KWML cycle will arrange your thoughts in order.
Your efforts to recover from anxiety and depression will become more streamlined and make clearer sense.
Surely now you stand a better chance to make headway to overcome your condition.

At this point I realised that I had sufficient material to tackle my anxiety and depression.
I felt that my research thesis was complete as I was able to answer the questions I sought to investigate.

16

If you do this, then you are going to recover and see your life change

To avoid childhood paradigms and 4F responses, Dr Glover recommends acting in an integrated manner.
However, this would be insufficient because we also need to set the framework for our integrated mind to operate in.

This is where modelling comes into effect.

Identify a person who has successfully completed a similar goal to yours.

Read about their lives and pathway to success. Not only is it important to replicate their actions, but it is also vital to have the same mindset of these people for success.

Now that you can alter your emotions, and direct your efforts, it is now important to build a positive mindset.

NLP offers a positive mental attitude check list.

There are six common characteristics for people with a positive mental attitude.
1.   Ignite your inner motivation: Vividly imagine specific goals.

2. Recognise the value of high standards: Your attitude must not be anything less than what is acceptable (No mention of being perfect).

3. Set bitesize goals. Focus on one goal and break it down step by step.
    Think in terms of bite size chunks by focusing on small tasks that you can do now.
    Gain satisfaction from completing each small step with specific measurable chunks.

4. Reframe your concept of time. Cultivate the ability to view ideas and tasks without time constraints.

5. Personal involvement.
    Increasing our personal commitment intensifies our focus.
    We need to play a part in our own success.
    We must act for our own welfare rather than delegate our responsibilities to others.
    This will empower us to take bolder actions to build our future.
    Take actions for ourselves no matter how small they may seem., unless you require a specific skill and must hire an expert.

6. Self-to-self comparison
    This is how you judge yourself and involves the magician quadrant. Don't fall into the habit of comparing yourself with others.

Ask: "How far have I progressed since yesterday, last week, last year?" Learn to measure your own progress with your own development, and assume that you knew you couldn't fail.
Look only at your own progress and measure yourself with yourself.

The only time you pay attention to other people is when their accomplishments and successes tells us that it is possible for a person to do it. If one person can do it, then anyone can.

17

But what about if I change my mind or fall off? Then follow this

Dr Charles Garfield in 'Peak performers: The new heroes of American business' shows that there are common key characteristics to perform at your peak.

I then compared the KWML quadrants to his list.

Key characteristics:

King 1:   Commitment to a mission larger than themselves. Vision.

Warrior 2: Purposeful activity with real measurable results. Goal setting and targets.

Magician 3: Team building, course corrections, flexible paths, and changes in mindset/management (tactics).

Lover 4:   Changing with the times, taking responsibility and not falling into addictions, and total belief in likelihood of own success (moving into warrior quadrant).

Once again, these characteristics are incredibly like the KWML model. *So, by learning the KWML model, then surely this will be the springboard that makes all the other traditional resources on anxiety, depression and fear easier to grasp and follow.*

18

Now that we are on the same page, what are you going to do next?

Through a process of reverse engineering this thesis shows that overcoming anxiety and depression is a real possibility.
Unlike traditional material suggests, I believe that anxiety and depression cannot be isolated to a single cause or strand of science.
It requires many moving parts that when put together forms a framework to overcome the condition.

By triangulating the material and teasing out trends and patterns, I formed an overall view of the causes and effect of anxiety and depression.
By using Carl Jung's King, Warrior, Magician, Lover archetype diagram, I applied a system that could help to overcome or at least alleviate anxiety and depression.

The METHOD A proposes a replicable procedure to consciously change your emotions and mental state to focus on a desired goal. Simultaneously, it will drive down your anxiety and depression.

Traditional therapy suggests isolating the condition by being positive. But as we see, being positive has many meanings to many people. What does be positive actually mean?

My method suggests using a positive force, a personal vision, to counteract anxiety and depression. This to me seems to be more sustainable and healthier.

If there is one single over-arching goal to aim for, then it would be to reach the centre of the KWML matrix, point O.
This has been my overall aim since putting these ideas into a book.

This is where you will be in a flow state. Flow state is when everything becomes effortless and time feels limitless. This is where balance is achieved.
People in flow state see the big picture allowing their minds to run free and allow creativity and talent to go where it is needed. Here, thoughts are not impeded with anxiety, depression and fear.

Earlier, I queried if there was a balance that could be achieved between negative chatter and focus.
I now believe that I have found a method that allows an individual to set the balance to any point they may wish.

In a nutshell, to overcome anxiety and depression you must:

1. Eliminate childhood paradigms.
2. Set a vision with clear goals.
3. Use The METHOD A to take action to meet your goals.

It is the interpretation of the KWML and its applicability to overcome anxiety and depression that sets this thesis apart from the rest of the material available for the condition.
Your success will depend on how you apply the KWML Matrix in your life.

If you have reached this far in my thesis then I know that you are a select few who are serious about overcoming their anxiety, depression and fear.
I'm sure that this thesis has made you think about your condition differently now, and offers renewed hope and a new approach.

This was my aim.

Your next step must be to re-read my thesis and go through the steps listed.

To assist you, I have referenced the most influential sources, so please check them out because it will help to re-enforce the material in the thesis and make things clearer.
If you replicate how I carried out my research you will no doubt make excellent headway.

At the start, I was unsure as to what I would find. All I wanted was to find some sort of guidance that would help me to overcome my anxiety, depression and fear.
My journey revealed a lot about myself and I learned how a healthy person should think and act.

What I did uncover changed my life.
The game changer is being able to reconcile theory with practical steps to achieve a specific outcome.

I never intended to publish this material, it was only notes for my personal use. But after speaking to many people with the condition, I realised that many topics in my thesis were still unknown to many anxiety and depression sufferers. I was thus convinced that my thesis could be of value to others.

In this thesis, you will be challenged, you will be motivated, and you will be inspired.

But more importantly, you will get practical ideas and strategies that will take you to the next level of your recovery and life in general.

This book is a life changer and I promise you, you won't regret it.

Publishing this thesis is my way of helping you overcome anxiety, depression and fear.

19

Where did all this information come from?

Primary sources

Steve Andreas and Charles Faulkner. (2009) The new technology of achievement. William Morrow & Co

Susan Jeffers. (2007) Feel the fear and do it anyway. Vermilion London.

Dale Carnegie. (2006) How to win friends and influence people. Vermilion London.

Dr Robert Glover. (2003) No More Mr. Nice Guy. Running Press. USA.

Aaron Gilies. (2018) How to survive the end of the world. Two Roads.

Susan Forward with Craig Buck. (2002) Toxic parents. Bantam Stephen R Covey. (1989) The 7 habits of highly effective people. Simon and Schuster.

Edward Bernays. (2012) Crystallizing public opinion. Snowball publishing.

Gustave Le Bon. The crowd. A study of the popular mind. Maestro reprints.

Psychotherapy:

Psychoanalytic theory https://youtu.be/iMkJ9vtn8jQ

Freud's psychosexual development | Individuals and Society | MCAT | Khan Academy https://youtu.be/nG7yosFQHP4

Sigmund Freud: Id, Ego, Superego- Psychodynamic- Psychoanalytic Personality Theory Explained https://youtu.be/1Vs8uE8_02E

PSYCHOTHERAPY - Sigmund Freud https://youtu.be/mQaqXK7z9LM

TEDx talks:

Hypnotize Yourself | Dan Candell | TEDxAuburnMiddleSchool https://youtu.be/BGbGpm7M12w

Change your mindset, change the game | Dr. Alia Crum | TEDxTraverseCity https://youtu.be/0tqq66zwa7g

What separates successful people from unsuccessful? | Claudiu Moldovan | TEDxYouth@Helsingborg https://youtu.be/ppbwElbRuiM

The art of being yourself | Caroline McHugh | TEDxMiltonKeynesWomen https://youtu.be/veEQQ-N9xWU

How to know your life purpose in 5 minutes | Adam Leipzig | TEDxMalibu https://youtu.be/vVsXO9brK7M

The Secret of Becoming Mentally Strong | Amy Morin | TEDxOcala https://youtu.be/TFbv757kup4

How to practice emotional hygiene | Guy Winch | TEDxLinnaeusUniversity https://youtu.be/rni41c9iq54

The big secret nobody wants to tell | Bruce Muzik | TEDxSinCity https://youtu.be/lkbWIfP3mLw

Isolation is the dream-killer, not your attitude | Barbara Sher | TEDxPrague https://youtu.be/H2rG4Dg6xyI

How Your Unconscious Mind Rules Your Behaviour: Leonard Mlodinow at TEDxReset 2013 https://youtu.be/vcJm-y7UnLY

Own Your Behaviours, Master Your Communication, Determine Your Success | Louise Evans | TEDxGenova https://youtu.be/4BZuWrdC-9Q

The Magic of Not Giving a F*** | Sarah Knight | TEDxCoconutGrove https://youtu.be/GwRzjFQa_Og

Free your mind to evolve faster: reboot, rewire & rethink | Scott Ely | TEDxNorthwesternU https://youtu.be/2hGjuvMBBj0

Neurohacking: rewiring your brain | Don Vaughn | TEDxUCLA https://youtu.be/xzbHtIrb14s

Flex your cortex -- 7 secrets to turbocharge your brain | Sandra Bond Chapman, Ph.D. | TEDxBayArea https://youtu.be/uUL5o-1Yawo

The lethality of loneliness: John Cacioppo at TEDxDesMoines https://youtu.be/_0hxl03JoA0

The Unstoppable Force - The Real Difference Between Success and Failure | Dan Lok | TEDxSFU https://youtu.be/qvNyo1-AK6o

The Invisible Force - self-image – enables you to achieve great goals | Dan Lok | TEDxStanleyPark https://youtu.be/C5dyGh3oMVQ

The Power of Zero Tolerance | Isabelle Mercier | TEDxStanleyPark https://youtu.be/--mY5ruEhqI

Natural Bodybuilding: Become the best version of yourself | Mischa Janiec | TEDxHSGhttps://youtu.be/CR5krXHkr2I

Why is Everyone So Fat, Broke and Busy? Jeff Gaines at TEDxAlbany 2010 https://youtu.be/GxJVbzdf5gI

Unwavering Focus | Dandapani | TEDxReno https://youtu.be/4O2JK_94g3Y

Breathe to Heal | Max Strom | TEDxCapeMay https://youtu.be/4Lb5L-VEm34

<u>Carl Jung Occult Lecture</u>

[Occult Lecture] How to Master Your Thinking-Patterns and Habits for Self-Development https://youtu.be/7xIXCKoihRs

[Occult Lecture] How to Deal with Stress and Depression Wisely for Self-Development https://youtu.be/K7Kwz6PKtMM

[Occult Wisdom Lecture] The Inner Mind and Outer Mind https://youtu.be/cYAWt4P1Dbo

How to Handle Your Anger for Self-Development [Occult Wisdom Lecture] https://youtu.be/vTnGz1KrpY8

Occult Lecture] How to Master Your Thinking-Patterns and Habits for Self-Development https://youtu.be/7xlXCKoihRs

[Occult Wisdom Lecture] How to Deal with This Chaotic World Wisely https://youtu.be/KlutCmHY0Eg

The Transcendent Function, by Carl Jung (full audio) https://youtu.be/bpk60CdAQ2A

[Occult Lecture] How to Master Your Thinking-Patterns and Habits for Self-Development https://youtu.be/7xlXCKoihRs

Carl Jung on Accepting the Darkness of Self and Other https://youtu.be/FvgmyaSTosg

Carl Jung - Approaching the Unconscious https://youtu.be/lViOY9wIDBQ

The Six Pillars of Self Esteem https://youtu.be/mfFUVnwCNVY

<u>Eckhart Tolle</u>

Eckhart Tolle - How to Stop Self Talk in the Head https://youtu.be/ig2lFXSMUjM

Eckhart Tolle - The state of no thought https://youtu.be/EFr-2z4Pzn8

How Do You Deal with Unconscious People? https://youtu.be/lqr98O8QT3M

How to take the right decision by Eckhart Tolle https://youtu.be/8GmkbhWhKS0

Better Your Life in 10 Minutes - Eckhart Tolle - Living in The Now/Present Moment https://youtu.be/KuzmVolsvMQ

How Do We Break the Habit of Excessive Thinking? https://youtu.be/dTFDfR47dl4

Where Do Our Thoughts Come From? https://youtu.be/rWFVi1cPUZo

I'm Aware of Fear That Is Almost Continually in Me https://youtu.be/L4os0IxmGv8

How to Let Go - Powerful Tools to Let Go of the Past & Negative Feelings https://youtu.be/Sg-OcYneVso

Hypnosis and meditation

Sleep Hypnosis Journey to Become Your Ideal Self (Inner Advisor, Relaxation, Confidence) https://youtu.be/fS_Yb0PtpKQ

Hypnosis for Clearing Subconscious Negativity https://youtu.be/FiPDV9L5qpQ

1 Hour Sleep Hypnosis: Higher Self-Healing for Depression & Anxiety https://youtu.be/HpHKf4tlvFw

Hypnosis for Meeting Your Spirit Guide in a Lucid Dream (Guided Meditation, Inner Adviser)https://youtu.be/ZxH0UEcMaFE

Meditation for Concentration, Anxiety, ADD, ADHD - How to Meditate for Beginners – BEXLIFE https://youtu.be/hzFOx0J9vXI

Guided Meditation for Detachment from Over-Thinking (Anxiety / OCD / Depression) https://youtu.be/1vx8iUvfyCY

Hypnosis for Men: Overcoming "Nice Guy" Syndrome (Confidence / Anxiety / Relationships) https://youtu.be/nRefcyPrhPM

Motivational videos:

Zig Ziglar - The Law of Attraction: Believe in Yourself https://youtu.be/f9V-J3hHrwo

Les Brown: How to Reprogram Your Mind (Les Brown Motivation) https://youtu.be/ETzy4UfR4yw

Jim Rohn - Psychology of Wealth Thinking (Jim Rohn Personal Development) https://youtu.be/ppUx4J3J9FY

Simon Sinek - FIND YOUR TRUE PURPOSE (Powerful Motivational Speech 2017) https://youtu.be/WBR29z50O-k

BEST SPEECH EVER - Secrets of humanity and happiness | MOST INSPIRING SPEECH https://youtu.be/oSSUM5UdPEc

Start with why -- how great leaders inspire action | Simon Sinek | TEDxPugetSound https://youtu.be/u4ZoJKF_VuA

Jordan Peterson's Life Advice Will Change Your Future (MUST WATCH) https://youtu.be/wqEsTPaUZF0

One of The Most Inspiring Speeches by Jim Kwik - The Power of Morning Routine | Facebook Depression https://youtu.be/o8ky8PDLBRw

Supporting resources:

The Psychology of Habits - One of The Most Motivational Speeches (life changing) https://youtu.be/vf2We-AEtmc

Dr. Isaiah Hankel: How Smart People Focus, Create, and Grow Their Way to Success https://youtu.be/h-5N0X7cdIs

Daniel Goleman on Focus: The Secret to High Performance and Fulfilment https://youtu.be/HTfYv3IEOqM

Steven Pressfield |The New Man Podcast with Tripp Lanier https://youtu.be/7p5yV3Bpspk

The Power of Indifference https://youtu.be/v3NGC9WUtG8

Gut bacteria and mind control: to fix your brain, fix your gut! https://youtu.be/mioR_WrkRaU

Heribert Watzke: The brain in your gut https://youtu.be/bkeBjP_9ZR4

Microbiome, Depression & Anxiety- Dr Milton Mills https://youtu.be/sv-j8cLPLQ0

How Gut Bacteria Affects Mood, Anxiety, and Weight https://youtu.be/cczfnvbPW4s

Rob Knight: How our microbes make us who we are https://youtu.be/i-icXZ2tMRM

Asleep in 60 seconds: 4-7-8 breathing technique https://youtu.be/gz4G31LGyog

How to Stop Ruminating https://youtu.be/KlpYu2938cs

How to Concentrate https://youtu.be/r_btfnCX0uo

HOW TO REPROGRAM YOUR SUBCONSCIOUS - Dandapani on London Reel https://youtu.be/Gku2OodrnQ0

<u>Websites:</u>

British Psychological Society https://www.bps.org.uk/

Society of Psychotherapy – A meeting place for friends of Psychotherapy https://societyofpsychotherapy.org.uk/

Association of Child Psychotherapists https://childpsychotherapy.org.uk/

The Jung Page – Home www.cgjungpage.org/

Sigmund Freud's Theories | Simply Psychology https://www.simplypsychology.org/Sigmund-Freud.html

Journal of Anxiety Disorders – Elsevier https://www.journals.elsevier.com/journal-of-anxiety-disorders

Publications | BPS - British Psychological Society https://www.bps.org.uk/publications